D0095181

Presented to

................................................

by

................................................

on

................................................

Published by Candle Books
an imprint of
**Lion Hudson plc**
Wilkinson House, Jordan Hill Road,
Oxford OX2 8DR, England
www.lionhudson.com/candle

ISBN 978 1 85985 990 2
e-ISBN 978 1 78128 121 5

First edition 2014

**Acknowledgments**
All scripture quotations, except those listed below, are taken or adapted
from the Contemporary English Version. Copyright © 1991, 1992, 1995
by American Bible Society. Used by permission.

Scripture quotations on pages 23 and 46 are taken or adapted from the
New Revised Standard Version Bible, copyright © 1989 National Council
of the Churches of Christ in the United States of America.
Used by permission. All rights reserved.

A catalogue record for this book is available
from the British Library

Printed and bound in China,
November 2013, LH17

# Prayers for Little Girls

Compiled by Juliet David
Illustrated by Julie Clay

CANDLE
BOOKS

This collection of age-appropriate prayers has been carefully designed for beginning readers.

Every prayer is closely based on Scripture.

Well-known and greatly loved Bible verses are included.

Most of the prayers are simple enough to repeat and memorize.

This book offers its young readers helpful first steps in prayer and praise.

J.D.

I pray to you, Lord!
Please listen when I pray
and hurry to help me.

PSALM 141:1

Our Lord and God,
you are worthy
to receive glory.

REVELATION 4:11

Lord, your word is a lamp
that gives light
wherever I walk.

PSALM 119:105

With all my heart
I praise you, Lord.

PSALM 138:1

# Praise Jesus
# now and forever!
# Amen

2 PETER 3:18

Lord, help me to do everything
without grumbling or arguing.

PHILIPPIANS 2:14

Let the mighty strength
of the Lord
make me strong.

EPHESIANS 6:10

Dear Lord,
Help me never get tired
of helping others.

BASED ON GALATIANS 6:9

I will sing
a new song to you,
O God.

PSALM 144:9

Hooray for God
in heaven above!

MARK 11:10

Dear Lord,
You asked fishermen
on the Sea of Galilee
to follow you.
Help me to follow you too.

SEE MARK 1:16–20

Lord,
Help me not to worry
about tomorrow.
You have told us
it will look after itself.

BASED ON MATTHEW 6:34

Lord,
Come and set up your kingdom,
so that everyone on earth
will obey you.

MATTHEW 6:10

Dear Father God,
Forgive me for doing wrong.
And help me to forgive others.

BASED ON MATTHEW 6:14

Dear Lord,
Help my light to shine
so that others will praise you.

BASED ON MATTHEW 5:16

Dear Lord,
I praise you
because of the wonderful way
you created me.

PSALM 139:14

Please listen, Lord,
and answer my prayer!

PSALM 86:1

Lord, make my heart glad!
My prayer is sincere.

FROM PSALM 86:4

Lord,
You are my mighty fortress,
and I depend on you.

PSALM 59:9

Dear Lord,
Don't let me follow evil ways.

PSALM 139:24

Lord,
Lead me in the way everlasting.

PSALM 139:24

Dear Heavenly Father,
Help me to guard my words
whenever I say something.

PSALM 141:3

When I pray,
Lord God,
I know for certain
you are with me.

PSALM 56:9

Dear Lord,
Even when I am afraid,
I keep on trusting you.

PSALM 56:3

Lord, we belong to you.
We tell you what worries us,
and you won't let us fall.

PSALM 55:22

Lord,
I will praise your name
because you are good.

PSALM 54:6

Listen, God, to my prayer!
Please listen and help me.

PSALM 55:1, 2

You are kind, God!
You are always merciful!
Please wipe away my sins.

PSALM 51:1

Let my words and my thoughts
be pleasing to you, Lord,
because you are my mighty rock
and my protector.

PSALM 19:14